D0003410

SMBSD
CPO

The
Knight Book

by Sue Dickson

Illustrations by Norma Portadino, Jean Hamilton, Chip Neville and Kerstin Upmeyer

Printed in the United States of America

Copyright © 1998 Sue Dickson
International Learning Systems of North America, Inc.
Oldsmar, FL 34677

ISBN: 1-56704-527-8 (Volume 16)

D E F G H I J K L M N—CJK—05 04 03 02 01 00

Table of Contents

Raceway Step 31

2

Did You Write to Santa ?

Vocabulary

1. wrap

2. wreath

3. write

4. written

5. writing

6. wrote

7. Wrinkles

wrist watch

8. wristwatch

9. wrong

10. wrench

11. who

12. whole

13. answer

3

"Holidays ! Holidays !" sang all the elves.

4

Time to take all the toys
down from the shelves;

Wrap pretty presents;

Hang up a green wreath;

Trim all the trees and put
trains underneath.

8

Dear Santa,
        I am writing to tell you who I am, and where I live. I hope you will bring me a truck.

I try to be good, and to keep my whole room neat. But it gets messy fast when I play with my dog Wrinkles. Please bring Wrinkles a whole box of Woofy Dog Chow.

Thank you, Santa
        Wi

Have you written to Santa ?
   If not, write today,
Ask him to put something
   nice in his sleigh.

Do you want a wristwatch or
some tools and a wrench ?

10

Or maybe a dolly that sits
on a bench ?

It's mine! I want the whole bagful!

Dear Aunt Ree,
Thank you for my birthday pres

If you wrote to Santa and
you have been good,

Not done things wrong but behaved as you should...

Then you'll hear from Santa. His answer will say:

"I'm glad you've been good.
Have a fine holiday !"

The End

The Brave Knight

Vocabulary

1. knight
2. knew
3. know
4. knock
5. knees
6. knapsack
7. knife
8. knit

9. knob
10. knowledge
11. known
12. knuckles
13. knot
14. kneel

Story Word

15. corn field
    cornfield

Tom was a brave
knight. The king knew
that Tom was brave.

One day the king called
Tom.

"Could you fight a
dragon ?" he asked.

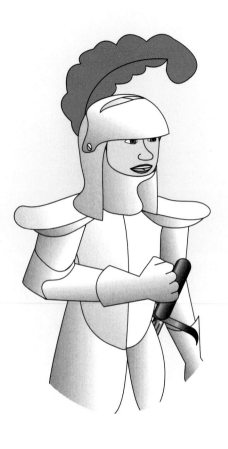

"Yes, I know how to fight a dragon," said Tom.

"I would hit him and knock him till he fell to his knees."

"Good," said the king. "You must do that."

"I will get ready now," said Tom.

18

Tom went home to pack
his knapsack. In went his
big knife. In went his
new yellow knit socks.

In went his club with the knob on top. In went his book of <u>Dragon Knowledge</u>.

20

Tom went to find the
dragon.

Soon he found him in
the king's cornfield.

Tom took his knife and
waved the yellow knit socks.

The dragon didn't know what to think!

Tom waved his club with
the knob on top. The
dragon did not want to be
hit on the nose . . .

or banged on his knuckles!

24

The dragon fell on his knees. Tom quickly tied **a big knot** in the dragon's tail.

"Don't hurt me," begged the dragon. "I know you have won."

Tom saw the dragon kneel. He knew that the dragon had given up the fight.

"If you don't hurt me, I will work for your king," yelled the dragon.

"Fine," said Tom.

"You must begin your work **now** !" said Tom.

So the dragon started to work in the king's cornfield.

28

Soon Tom took the king a bag of the best popcorn he had ever tasted !

The End

29

Sam and His Folks

Vocabulary

1. folks
2. yolk
3. half
4. calm
5. walk
6. walked
7. stalk
8. palm
9. should
10. would

11. could
12. salve
13. talk
14. talking
15. calf
16. salmon

Story Words

17. country
18. cat er pillar
    caterpillar

Sam went with his folks.
They drove in the car for
half the day. They drove
to the country.

They camped near a
big lake.

"Ah," said Dad. "Such a calm and peaceful place."

Sam and his folks
went for a walk.

Sam saw a caterpillar on a stalk.

It walked on Sam's palm. It tickled !

"Soon it will be a butterfly," said Sam. "Should I keep it ?"

"No, it should be free," said his folks.

Sam walked on a plant. It had three leaves. It made Sam itch. Sam felt bad.

The itch was on the calf of Sam's leg. Mom put salve on it. Salve stopped the itch.

Mom said, "That was poison ivy, Sam. It has three leaves. *'Leaflets three, let them be.'* Can you say that, Sam ?"

"Yes," said Sam.

39

The lake was calm. Dad and Sam went fishing.
"Sh," said Dad to Sam. "Talking could scare the fish !"

"Sh," said Sam to the
calf. "Don't talk !"

The Egg Yolk

Sam should get a fish
with this bait. Sam fished
and fished.

42

He waited and waited.
Would Sam get a fish ?
Could Sam get a fish ?

Yes, He **did !**

The End

44

Vocabulary

1. crumb
2. crumbs
3. numb
4. comb
5. lamb
6. bomb
7. dumb
8. doubt
9. doubted
10. climb
11. plumber
12. limb
13. debt

45

Red Robin sat on his limb. He was getting cold.

Red was tired. Tired of digging worms. *Tired* of hunting for crumbs.

"My toes are numb!"

"I don't like cold and snow. I will go south," said Red.

Red packed his bag.
He put in his last few
crumbs.

He put in his comb
and brush. He put in his
toy lamb.

50

"Good-by, good-by, cold
weather! Sunshine, here
I come!" he called.

51

Just as the first snow
began to fall, Red Robin
made his lift-off!

Red flew and flew, and
the cold wind blew!

53

A big wind smacked
Red. It hit him like a
bomb !

Poor Red ! He could
not fly. He hurt his wing
and his left thumb, too.
He doubted that he could
get to the South.

Poor Red !
He hopped along the road.
He was cold.
He was numb.
His crumbs
were all gone.

And the road stretched on and on.

What would Red do ?

What could Red do ?

If a bird cannot fly,
can a bird get a ride ?

screech

That is just what Red did!
He waved and waved.
Soon a truck stopped for
him... **screech**!

"Climb in," said the man.
"I'm a plumber, you see.
I'll make you a limb.
You can ride here with me."

60

"Thank you," sang Red.
"I'm glad that we met.
I'll sing you sweet songs
To pay off my debt."

Red came to the South,
And his numb toes were
warm.
Red was not dumb.
He had weathered the
storm !

The End

Can a Gnat Gnaw ?

Vocabulary

1. gnat
2. Gnatsville
3. sign
4. as sign ment
   assignment
5. gnash
6. gnashed
7. gnaw
8. gnawed
9. gnawing
10. gnawer
11. gnu
12. resign

The Gnatsville Gazette

Notice:
We need strong gnats.
Go to the Acorn Forest if
you want a job. Look for
the sign. Good Pay!

"Oh, boy! Let's go!"

66

Listen !
Her Honor,
the Ant Queen !

Vocabulary

Silent K̸

1. honor
2. honest
3. hour
4. John
5. Thomas

Silent t̸

6. listen
7. whistle
8. bristle
9. castle
10. moisten
11. hustle
12. bustle

13. glisten
14. fasten
15. hasten
16. gristle
17. thistle
18. often
19. rustle

---

qu=k

20. bouquet
21. antique
22. croquet

23. boutique
24. mosquito
25. mosquitoes

68

Listen ! The Ant Queen is blowing her whistle !

She's shouting out orders... "Get a brush with good bristles !"

"Scrub up this castle!
Moisten those stamps!

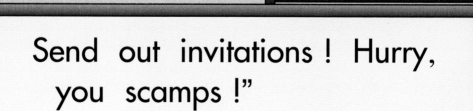

Send out invitations! Hurry,
you scamps!"

"The dining room table must have a bouquet,

And bring little cookies upon a gold tray.

Light up the antique lamps on every wall.

Rush now, you workers, both large ants and small."

"Take out my jewels where they're hidden from sight.

You're on your honor to do the job right !"

"Now polish those jewels till
they glisten like new!
Don't take an hour, and
when you are through,

You must fasten the curtains
with new golden chains!

Close all the windows in
case that it rains!"

"Hasten to set up a game
   of croquet,

For soon after dinner,
   King John likes to play."

"Now, go to the kitchen !
You must make a treat !

And be sure no gristle
is cooked with the meat !"

"Make King John's bed
with his thistle-down quilt.

I know he's been camping
in sand and in silt."

"Run to the Bug Boutique!
Buy me a gown!

I shall look grand
when King John comes
to town."

"Listen !!! Mosquitoes !!!
Listen ! Stand Guard !

Don't let those strange bugs
come into our yard !"

Such a hustle and bustle
  you never have seen!
So many orders from
  such a small queen!

What's going to happen
  in this tiny yard?
It isn't so often
  an ant-queen works hard!

79

Do I hear a rustle outside in
the grass ?
Is that a small army beginning
to pass ?
And who is that riding the
big golden horse ?
It's the Queen's husband ! It's
King John, of course !

The End